BROKEN
ANGELS

by

SUSANNA ROXMAN

1

BROKEN ANGELS

This edition published in 1996-7
by Dionysia Press
20A Montgomery St
Edinburgh EH7 5JS

Set by Dionysia Press

Cover design by Thom Nairn

ISBN: 0 9522341 1 4

Dionysia Press would like to express thanks to the Scandinavian
Arts Foundation for financial assistance in the publication of this
collection.

Printed in Scotland by Dionysia Press

for Isis

ACKNOWLEDGEMENTS

Most of the poems in this collection originally appeared in American publications such as **Oxford Magazine, Roanoke Review, Sanskrit, Soundings East, The Spoon River Poetry Review, Webster Review, Westview, Writers' Forum, Elk River Review, Sidewalks, Visions International,** and **Voices International**.

Some were published in **New Contrast** (South Africa), **Odyssey** (Britain), **Poetry Halifax Dartmouth** (Canada), **Poetry Kanto** (Japan), **Ramraid Extraordinaire** (Britain), **Understanding** (Scotland), **Whetstone** (Canada), and other literary journals.

Others have appeared in the following anthologies:

Broken Dreams, edited by Robert W. Olmsted. Conservatory of American Letters/Northwoods Press, 1992 (USA).

1994 Dan River Anthology, edited by Richard S. Danbury. Conservatory of American Letters/Dan River Press, 1994 (USA).

Alabama River Rendezvous, edited by John Curbow. Curbow Publications, 1996 (USA).

"Ithaca" received an Editor's Choice prize from **Elk River Review** (USA; the Marjorie Lees Linn Poetry Award, 1994) and was published in an Award Issue of this journal. "Concentration-Camp Guard Found Dead in a Canal" got the same prize, in the same competition, in 1995, and appeared in the Award Issue of **Elk River Review** next year.

"Seaside Resort opposite Elsinore, in February" got a special mention in the Open University Poetry Competition, 1994.

"Destination: Damascus" and "Lapland" each received an Honourable Mention in the **Alabama River Rendezvous** Contest, Curbow Publications, in 1995, and were published in that book.

CONTENTS

I

II

III

IV

I

OLD EXECUTIONERS

retired executioners
have hands rounded like horn-spoons
as if they'd often held
rain-plumped prize roses,
babies' heavy heads
or unusually large drinks

elongated ears
and cheeks are sewn
softly of chamois
registering nothing
                eyelids
unfold as napkins, lips
part above rounded plates

old executioners
if you leave them alone
live eventlessly and long,
an afternoon which leans across the lawns,
and safely tucked in at last
hold rounded bellies high

no screams will tear
curtains from rings
                no stench
of excrement disturb
the turn of rounded years

THE PEAT-BOG

Here you may rehearse immortality
of a kind, if you dare
get thoroughly tanned, like hides
in a container of urine.

Here you might sacrifice
coins or choice jewels
to brown space, if you care,
touching up the chiaroscuro.

You're bound to encounter
the mild-handed Bog Man
who still wears his hooded coat,
proof against history and rain.

He'd been ready for long when he went.
A bribe for this high-risk zone,
he was hanged with a length of rope,
then tipped into the sheer Unknown.

His milk-smooth forehead
allows you to decipher nothing
denoting emotion, only
an angle of utter consent.

CONCENTRATION-CAMP GUARD FOUND DEAD IN A CANAL

"Could swim. Was armed."

Three feet into the mirror
and three from the brambled edge,
he moves with a breathing feather

where white rings widen on sepia.

Cambric-tea light softens both lips,
but darkness puts coins on his eyelids,

rests under willow-roots and tongue.

This was the point where fears met,
hair now by air-bubbles bleached, the hand
an almost surfacing lily.

Black circles expand on the fading
canal. A shoal of steel nails

shivers across pockets and belt,

is gone. The water lies open
like a newspaper over his face.

BROKEN ANGELS

the air is full of them,
up to no good,
constantly falling,
hair and jackets
on fire

                 nobody
wants them, fatherless
angels, featherless,

tracing a trail
of blood along the sky:

not open enough
for the garden or stagnant
yet for the pit,

each wears a china face,
too beautiful
for tears or smiles:
the tiny beard
seems glued on for fun

mouth so diminutive
it could barely devour
a cocktail-cherry,
                 eye-whites
tinged with blue,
clarity begun
at home, calm
of forest lakes
                yet grace
must still look so;

soft and swift,
these boys raise
machine-guns like palm-leaves
or present a stiletto,
Annunciation lily
outlined against golden
fretwork

        perpetual
outsiders, dreaming
of implosion, disaster,
though no one's messengers,
they carry a bulletin
of ashes

        those upper
gods unmoved,
they turn to the lower,

shun yellow
bellowing trumpets,
the only noise
bullets eating
bone and plaster;

conceived in sin,
on the wrong side
of every wall,
they beat their knuckles
raw on all
pearl-gates:
        nobody
shouted "Come in"

SURVIVORS

gathering with sallow finger-printed faces
around one tallow dip,
listening not for the helicopter
but a message, some explanation,

survivors don't smile:
they stare ahead, through walls,
across their steaming soup, the small,
thoughtfully provided whiskies

frost will cling to eyebrows now
even jasmined afternoons

though survivors missed
the experience as well as its meaning,
they had prepared against a revelation,
pillar of superior furred light
simply occurring

survivors trusted serendipity
the way a Siberian husky relies
on driver and end of trek:
what happened was emptiness without frontiers,
no terror was granted, just a blank expanse

survivors can't forget
what never happened,
lookalikes turned into herms
of frozen flesh, fangs bared,
but friendly, almost company
on the glass verge of nothing

survivors won't flatter
with a speech, bottle or bouquet
                                    they feed

on guilts, any relief
laced with frustration, a sense
of being *de trop*, then panic
at 4 p.m. when whiteness breaks

GOTHIC POEM

It's pathetic, your wish to bury
yourself some smudged afternoon:
the oblong of gravel, the outsize
lilies. Like Ophelia's, your end
is doubtful. Stooping mourners
scrunch up hankies in fists,

reel off expected clichés
about our common lot, as if death
were a habit that couldn't be broken.
Your disclosed stone points out:
"Here lies that person
who I was." The sound of clods

drives you frantic: you jump down
(compare Hamlet or Heathcliff),
tear open the lid
to worship your face with kisses.
"It's mine still." Shocked
relatives help you to a taxi.

Perpendicular, you grow at night
from your grave, arms folded
demurely as Giselle's. But soon
even this imitation
of your form and force will self-destruct
into wistful mist. *Requiescas.*

AUX MORTS

A matter of line and slow motion,
softly folding legs, *pliés* and *fondus*,
arms freezing into pointed snowdrop-vaults
or duveted under dew.

Something like the Jugend style perhaps,
tendriled hands, lean curves of tendon
and bone decaying, boles in a fever swamp.

Texture might be one suggestion,
mulch squelching, marble slabs
turning marshmallow-tender, or a massive
but melting pair of silver sugar-tongs.

No cure for love or winter, just some cold
comforts, pearls half dissolved in acid
and gently parachuting snow.

BALLAD OF A BALLOONIST

The blue polyester is already pregnant,
displaying some sponsor's name.

In this thickening dusk
there's the quiet roar of a gas-flame.

The passenger takes nobody with him.
His hands shine on the wicker edge.

This morning was normal.
It isn't that he doesn't like it here.

We strike poses on both sides.
He bought few if any roses for his wife.

Such solitary flights can't be so bad
except that you might get lost,

never heard from again.
He's dumping sand-bags like dead pigs.

The stiff ropes untied,
we offer honey-water and milk.

If the takeoff gives him a kick
he's careful not to show it.

Winds may drive him where no one guessed,
blue tigers leaping from nowhere.

He rises at an acute or obtuse angle,
gliding as an angel along the lawn.

Though he controls his altitude
he can't choose to turn left or right.

17

It's difficult to discern him now,
  tossed by cross-currents.

His balloon charges like a blue cow
  through the universe.

We're told he hopes to descend
on the other side of tonight.

II

INTERIOR WITH A KITCHEN-MAID

Words have grown solid here:
jug, ladle, bowl.
She blows on a spoonful of dreams.

Light creams down every day
till veins rise on cleaned boards
and a pink blur indicates

an afternoon of copper-pots.
The dresser hoards almonds
and raisins in its brown pocket.

Acts have proved valid here,
filling life to the brim.
Lemons and smooth loaves

turn cheeks towards window-panes
blue as milk. Veins rise
again on her competent hands

that could peel a pear most
elegantly, the unbroken spiral
sinking with a slight sigh.

The calm and keenness of her face,
like *crème de menthe,* reveal
nothing of deep submission

on this very table, nocturnal
orgies, cheese and cake
filling that hole where once

her self-respect used to perch,
or how she gutted five rabbits, the stain
still so ingrained it won't scrub off.

THE SALT LICK

In moonlight it curves like marble
chiselled by a master.

Plunging tongues of cattle
scooped out each cardinal point,

constructed a central massif,
madly glittering Mont Blanc.

Cows leave plenty behind,
their legacies and proofs,

rough hairs barbing a wire,
soft loaves raisined with flies

or dry droppings, nourishing
as muesli and pierced with tall stalks.

A glint of sky enamels
freshly minted hoof-prints.

Cities were once commissioned
where a cow had condescended to rest,

her fragrant glistening mattress
becoming a sacred place.

Creation in Norse myth starts
with a heifer boldly licking

cosmic frost into flesh.
In the beginning was the Cow.

GEORGIA O'KEEFFE

The process of trial and terror
yielded an unwieldy insight,
that she became everything she saw,
thin cross and pagan mountains.

Skull of cow or dismembered bull
and a butterfly marking its forehead,
starkness borrowed from deserts,
joy of corolla and sepals,

sepia and burnt sienna
checking the euphoria, gold or mauve,
all this was her responsibility.

The fear didn't spring from emptiness,
such vastness of unused landscapes:
she recognized their solitude as hers.

Nor (she frowned) some rather obvious imagery,
the *memento mori* foundering in sand
or pansies as miniature death's-heads.

And that gender-bound temptation, to prettify
(oh satin convolutions of the rose),
she'd overcome already in her youth
with little conscious effort.

It was the garden-bound softness
opening like a kiss to sun or snow,
a slow silken sinking
without resistance, an effacement of will

early at night or in the dusk
just before dinner:
                    gravel and rocks,

even scattered bones upset her less
than this patient abdication into plush.

ALLEGRA

Pigeons cook porridge under eaves.
Ropes make marks on the mossed well-head.

Her palms and nose flatten a window
while voices trace arches of plainsong in the air.

These brown smells are leather and polishing wax.
The breeze is leafing through paper poplars.

Stained glass panes filter the past.
This cobbled close remains empty.

Children's faces float like leaves
discarded on the bottomless water of cisterns.

A freckled sister brings cake and an apple.
Roads will deepen with white dust.

Papa lives in a silver locket.
Bells turn up their pouting mouths.

Sometimes at dawn a seascape enters,
showing that the wonderful always exists.

Swifts may pass, migrating north.
From a lace-shawl the wraith of perfume rises.

At sunset angels rustle in the orchard,
pink wings tipped with ink.

A rose without scent lies in a Bible.
A china cheek presses hard against flesh.

*Note. Allegra was Lord Byron's and Claire Clairmont's
daughter. She was placed in an Italian convent where
she died, about five years old.*

CHAMBER MUSIC

The penultimate year took place in penumbra.
Prisms tinkled in a minor key.

Bed-tombs provided interrupted slumber.
Bay-windows kept the world at bay.

Brown stayed the predominant colour.
It was usually Sunday afternoon.

Here I became a resident scholar
of domestic vices. From the gloom

I watched shadows growing
like Virginia creepers on bricked city walls.

The heaviness of mahogany proved my undoing.
A pregnant walnut chest of drawers

was never delivered. This house had been cluttered
with unwieldy nouns but few verbs.

At dusk the panes of a cupboard
would suddenly grimace, disturbed

by clocks bleeding time. A tub rested
on eagles' claws. Coagulated lace

on furniture showed how many years I'd wasted.
Parquet floors lay darkening with tacit rage.

III

INSIGHTS

there's always one day when you know
without having been told
before anything is confirmed

it's obvious in spite of this
from how the light slants
like a plank against a wall
or from a certain dryness in the air

an insight recorded
between heart-beats
between breaths

that moment when water unobtrusively
toughens into ice

OCTOBER

Take nothing for granted,
only this raw earth, turning.

Flesh from a freshly torn
apple gleams white with cold,

snow in your fist. Sharp
distances, absences form.

There's a scent of curry and transience,
a sense of steep sleep like a well.

Falling backwards from sun
you count your losses aloud.

Shadows of blank seasons
flutter past in a flock.

Your house has emptied. Each window
shuts, giving nothing back.

LAPLAND

Fog curdles into reindeer
soaring an inch or so

above ground before they melt,
emanations from a grey plateau.

It styles itself a mountain, then blurs,
becoming clouds and fluid concepts.

Rain bordering on snow
falls horizontally. Greyness

grows incarnate, though flesh dissolves
in this place of old hallucinations.

Here darkness means milk
and all criteria prove invalid.

I breathe on the moon till it mists
but a rock throws its pointed

head back and howls. It's a landscape
that almost doesn't exist.

IN THE LAPLAND MOUNTAINS

Cairns guarding fords are sitting cats.
At this altitude I don't know the correct attitude.
In a hut we buy baby loaves, flat
hands rejecting favours. We've lost our connections

back, seen bridges washed away, passes crammed
with blue snow. Everything is pushed to some edge.
Raw silk of water hangs from sills.
I write: "This vertical tendency, a Gothic trembling

skywards, vertigo . . . " What I think is: "Those drifts
                                                left
on banks look like thick soiled pancakes."
The current is worrying a reindeer's vertebra, turning
it over and over. Only small smells

rise, one of moisture, one green
and brown of soil. I hold a cold spoon.
Could ambitions bloom at this lichened latitude,
in such weather? Mountains open on hinges.

Then sleep sneaks up, a child who plucks at my sleeve.

ULTIMA THULE

Snow-grains keep drifting under eyelids.
The gale hits heavily, an axe.

Hibernating, my mind curls up
at nightfall, everything suspended.

Only the glacier crowfoot of blown
glass dazzles this arctic starkness.

Hammer iron into solid clouds.
Occasionally a solitary raven

crosses the void. Women's voices
are wailing in wind, men's

muttering in brooks. A mineral ice-block
displays its burning green heart.

No honeysuckle garlands this July,
no apples will burnish the cheeks of September.

Boulders lie split with knives. Falling
snow whispers, close to the bone.

THE LAPLAND HUT

We pass along a path, polished
by pawfall of wolves and winds.

At nightfall we find a hut
distinct like a dream in this orchard

where no branches blossom, only
reindeer's antlers turn blanched.

The door lacks a lock. We enter
without knocking, soaked,

barely sheltering against stars,
merely surviving, huddled together.

Others have stayed here before.
They left gifts against winter:

a matchbox, a twist of salt, biscuits.
These people warmed our berths,

pailed water from the same river,
will have named against odds

a provisional home, ad-libbed answers
and gods against the dark.

We add our marks in the guest book
to those already there.

Against cold we share sacred
fire and freeze-dried food.

Before breaking up against snowfall
at noon, we place on the sill

presents for later trekkers: bread,
a lighter, a scroll of birch-bark,

and think, sweeping the satined
floor: "They'll know that we care."

THE CAIRN

You see it before you can touch it.
Landmarking your mind, it provides
a convenient point of reference
though at close quarters
it doesn't look all that remarkable,
just a heap of rocks,
some dark and mossed,
others drier, crumbling
in daylight, like fairy-tale treasure.

But without this ugly monument
on its ridge you'd be totally lost,
so you add, as tradition bids,
one more stone
to the multitude, doing your bit
for people who'll surely pass
the same way later.
You sit down for a while, pouring
coffee from your heart-shaped flask,

then walk serenely on.

MOUNTAIN TREKKING

This is the way I see us: hand in hand,
two children, a greensilver lake,
some landscape hard to enter.

We're always here.
It's so far north that violets blow yellow
and, before morning, sugar-plums form drifts.

Our path has dwindled in the distant valley;
behind it, the magnificence of snows,
their solitary scent.

Now that you've left I understand
how close we are. Your image
never stopped walking by my side.

The grid of reindeer-fence means nothing,
cliffs and these clouds move in and out.
A pair of buzzards miaow.

I know you're gone to look for the new fall.
May Cassiopeia bless your tent,
cloudberry-hunting bears be gentle.

Wherever you coax a fire, remember me
who shared your trek, deep in another season,
a dreamless longed-for sleep.

ABOVE THE TREE-LINE

Solitude begins among clouds rising
from pebbles, fjelds descending from the sky.
They brush against past pain but let it go.
   The wind whistles through its teeth

in a vastness too serious for ghosts.
Verdigris rosettes of lichen are the only
flowers here, stones the sole fruit
   ripening. Your life is tried

and much might be discarded. Pick your way
with caution. Snow perforates the air
above green-grey pewter lakes on this level
   where joy at last will occur.

SEASIDE RESORT OPPOSITE ELSINORE, IN FEBRUARY

A place with everybody gone.

Smells of seaweed and wet sand on the wind,
resin on the breath.

Late snow ermining the outdoor stairs,
a beacon beckoning from Hamlet's castle.

The Sound kept moving past,
indifferent and busy.

Here one couldn't be in error
for long or even doubt.

How you draped the mirror
with a towel every morning
to protect me against narcissistic spleen.

Grey waves like backs of seals aimed south

and among pines I sensed the presence
of my father's benign ghost.

Days without edges,
pillows too deep for dreams,
one window yellow beside the shifting floor

a season when most things turned trivial.

The whispering winter garden
displayed one linen table under fronds,
one pale sail unfurling.

What you said here, that I should aspire
to something higher than acclaim.

Glass walls melted into twilight and rain.

Then our beginning of freedom, of wild wings,
geese noising high above us in the dark.

ANNUAL RINGS

I stand wrapped in clear wood.

My mind ripples endlessly, water
thinking in all directions at once.

I breathe with green and orange wings.

Quilted when brocade years flowed,
sandpapered by dry lunations,
I am concentric rings.

Any cross-section would show me
    wild, tigered.

I'm somebody's biography turned solid.

   Rains will spare
my pure astonished core.

White fire from the sky
I'd receive as an insight overdue.

Everything else, like sap in April,
filters quietly into mass.

There have been no losses,
    even of dignity.

   I have become
all I lived through.

STORM WARNING

clouds roaring by like trucks
double tyres on tarmac

all passages cancelled
the wind tearing its rubber sock

a darkened lighthouse, still sitting alert,
sucking its red and white lollipop

knock after knock, shock upon shock,
the pontoon finger-printing its puddles

breakers leaping like oil-fed flames
nibbling wood, making smoke

green as copper the sea
pounding on a locked steel door

WINTER

The flesh is willing.
All this winter still goes on.

Your hand lingers
on the rough gate.

Yesterday the sun was fingering
a tall angular throne.

Stones move in circles.
All the conspiracies are going on.

You make strong coffee,
invent charms against silence.

A year stands ajar,
about to open or close.

Your palms remember his back,
arched and slightly moist.

He never locked a rose
inside a mirrored cage.

All the disinformation still goes on.
Walk on the white bay,

wait for a quiet stranger
possibly into pain.

You cultivate rocks and stars.
Thirst will remain.

All the debriefing still goes on.
Blessed are those without regrets.

LIKE WINTER

The end of any epoch
looks like winter,
the end of spells.

I can smell no wetness, no mud.
Foregrounded twigs shine with electrum.
In the middle distance branches loom like lead.

Nudity enters and solitude.
Compulsory griefs
have multiplied, a mirror trick.

(These lavish deprivations: the relief.)

My most distinct image
is a tall peeling wall
sidelit by the low sun,

each scar and blister sharply drawn.
Pink and beige bricks
are finally beginning to show.

A name such as "Theophrastus"
may flit by like a magpie
reflected in a window opposite.

Then the long wait for snow.

IV

WRITTEN BY PAVLOV'S FEW, SAD, LAST SURVIVING DOGS

Ageing dogs, shabby dogs,
shaggy and darkened like last year's haycocks,
we cannot forget what we were:
golden tangible proofs;
pioneers of the Surface.

How could we get over our puppyhood
in that garden of pale tiles
and stainlessly spouting steel fountains:
the Pavlovian Institute.

With what nostalgia we remember
the assistants' footfall at dusk,
their friendly bell, the vibrations
of their gong, a brazen full moon,
and all at once
that perfect service, those delicious dishes,
fragrance of porridge and pie,
crunching of toast and rusk.
Our tails were happy then, our ears elated,
our salivation made a lake.

Now not even a bone to split,
not even gristle to chew.

The Master gave up reporting,
became an object himself.
His coat doesn't bulge or billow.
The ghost of sugar clings to its cuffs.

A bell still buzzes, a gong clangs,
but there is nothing to follow,
no footsteps, no key in the lock.
Above all the succulent dinners are gone.

44

Pathetic, obedient, we sit waiting as before,
conditioned to believe in a sequence,
in causality, matter, and motion.
We're caged in a fallacy, *ergo propter hoc.*
We dabble in theories, dribble on the floor.
Our silver saliva is creating an ocean.

To stop reacting correctly
must be the last and slowest thing to learn.

ONE POINT OF VIEW

Before we leave,
the gorgeous entertainer pulls off her wig,
blond as an iceberg.
She peels off her green finger-nails,
casually dropping them one by one
like emptied pods.
Her icicle heels deserted, she feels
with naked pads the expanse of stage,
its dust and draughts.

Silver-blue and spangled as a herring,
her evening gown comes next. Unzipped,
it's shed like an outgrown lifestyle.
Her bra is removed, its rubber balls
tossed, two apricots, into spectators' laps.

Wearing an ancient pair of jeans bled grey,
a tousled boy emerges with a smile.
He's glittering with perspiration,
these lights and our surprise.
Only his gaudy make-up stays
like a superstitious belief.

Yes, Beauty has been female for too long.
Let's dismantle her,
strip off her finery.
That show is over.
We're glutted with its kitsch.

Let's watch him as he truly is.

PUNCH

(a photograph by Hans van Manen)

Brandishing his fist like a discus or spear,
this live man ends and sums up an avenue
of poised metal or marble objects: he's Life
    pastiching Fine Art.

His punch shammed, the apparent movement a pose
(you may note that his weight is placed too far back),
he's arrested in mid-air, Zeno's arrow
    never arriving.

The down-turned face implies that Platonic Form
has descended as an avalanche, crushing
individual traits. This boxer incarnates
    rarefied beauty.

Exercise or anorexia pared his flesh
to polished points. Although eroticism shines
faintly from his chest, buttock, thigh, he remains
    trapped in a bronze trance.

SELF-PORTRAIT

Crossing what must have been the park,
wearing, I believe, black high-heeled sandals
and a very short shiny summer dress,
my hair falling down my waist,
I wasn't considering appearances.
With my conqueror's soul I was marching
in the platinum brilliance of a noon
which also belonged to Alexander, to Caesar.
I was only afraid of sand, insignificance.

Then the voice of a stranger: "Excuse me,
please allow me to say this:
you're the most beautiful woman I ever saw."
I woke up with a start.
But smiling, I replied with perfect ease,
every inch a lady: "Thank you,
what a lovely compliment."
He bowed and passed.

My unreal existence, all these
forced courageous marches through the world,
myself undaunted by ambushes, javelins, blizzards,
seasoned by decades of sieges and pitched battles,
disguised as a pretty woman.

V

ITHACA

Yes, that was how you returned,
on long shipwrecks.

In love with homecoming, wholeness,
you'd worn out the slowest war

but brought no gold or glamour,
simply the gift of revenge.

They didn't expect you back.
It could have been more convenient.

Only the dog neglected
your histrionic disguise.

Stones shone in your beginning
where you and the world overlapped.

Now time holds you by the throat,
shaking you like a rabbit.

Your dreams are gorged
with white limbs disappearing.

Once you called yourself *No One*.
This is the enduring ache,

to know against burnt sunsets
you should have stayed away.

IN THE TEMPLE OF HERCULES

How I keep coming back to this temple
of Hercules at Cadiz, his muscles well-defined
like terms in Euclidean geometry,
a hero turned into the symbol of sheer strength,
blindly powerful, in fact at times quite mad,

where also a terracotta statue stood
of Alexander, hair carefully curled,
eyes widened with horizons
and averted in a preoccupied manner,

the unreliable anecdote in Suetonius
providing a hypersensitive Caesar
whose tears coin-marked the mosaic floor:

Alexander, at his own present age,
having mastered so large a part of the world,

while Caesar, by contrast, had achieved nothing much
but mutual orgasms with innumerable women
(some terracotta breasts and buttocks well remembered)
and a few men.

                    My own age
was never approached by Alexander.

How I keep coming back to this temple:
Caesar's throat and toga damp with grief,
his almost sexual ache to count! to matter!
demonstrating to the indifferent how mistaken they were
and projecting the self into endless future fields,
an evening shadow pointing over grass.

Alexander named a city after his horse.
Caesar erected a statue of his horse.
Say what you like, at least these acts were worthwhile.

THE FALL OF THE REPUBLIC

Door within door within door
open, an endlessly receding vista,
   year within year.

   Between her palms
she can create an empty space
   shaped like a heart.

Walls peel, wells run dry:
   all decisions
were made long ago by other people.

   During a spell of summer
   she exists,
its clouds big with omens,
the sun in Leo placing
one paw on her egg-shell skull

while weeds run to seed,
civil conflicts grow rampant
among casually rambling roses.

Cawing, whistling, screeching birds
faintly scratch the silence.

She's familiar with heart-shaped jars,
emptiness coaxed into vases,
knows well her straw-pale windows

where bright mites of dust
sink, rise, turn,
beans boiling in slow pots,

but out of the corner of her mind
she registers balusters, busted

and waisted, remembers dolls,
considers this betrayal by the seasons,
how frescoes like petals fade,
chunks of masonry and mosaic
lie where they have fallen on long lawns.

Her slight straight figure hesitates,
locked in a block of shade.

Cypresses and frugal gravel
cut off her view. She believes
history is always executed elsewhere.

The glassy heavens should revolve around
her sundial in the middle of this garden.

When her stola disturbs the terrace,
thoughts and insights, tendrils,
accidentally catch hold of her sleeve or hem:

listening for the rumbling drums
of thunder, distant armies,
she'll soon see autumn returning
    with expected urns

but once she wove one coat every year
    for an absent man:
    loyal as the swallows,
she kept worrying her loom.

Even her passionate waiting seems dated.

    At her gate the wind
sniffs loudly, then throws
its head back and howls.

There's a constant sense of doom,
of some inexplicable impending misfortune.

Birds wheel, stray, her hair
strays from its chignon, also the wind
will stray, restless, chasing its own tail,

then claws and beaks attack her composure
and at nightfall stars stab her with pins,
her hand groping for the moon's windfall.

Half chosen, half imposed her solitude:
    she sags, crucified
on this horizontal beam of time,
the vertical bar of place.

Her months don't move slowly
    or cyclically any longer
        but faster and faster,

a mute acceleration into disaster.

DESTINATION: DAMASCUS

On the stark plain, there it happened,
and it stood like bronze.

In the green morning, then it was,
each star slipping through your fingers.

You'd always dabbled in respectability,
seen sand rubbing the public images.

Dust was densing as you began to move
from one arbitrary point to another.

Sesame seeds between your teeth,
you were fingering profits and losses.

It could have taken place in any place
where only sand-roses bloom.

You were overwhelmed,
fell reluctantly, surprised and terrified

like somebody hit with a rock.
Sand walked past.

Your life split in two,
before and after.

There's no forgetting This,
no use thinking you made it all up.

Afterwards you were thirsty.
The wind ran its fingers through your hair

and you were not the enemy any more.
You don't know how to name it

but This remains your one frame of reference,
your only norm,

sand sealing your eyes,
chafing your hands and feet.

Though you're now, years later,
at it again, clutching dogmas

but of a different kind,
This will keep.

PONTIUS PILATE

He passed through the gate into Gaul.

At this almost civilized hour
he watches the terse hills

where his day stiffens like a sentry.
Suspended from one hair

the river gleams and becomes a sword.
T:s of wood spread-eagle the vines.

His wife sleeps calmly: she's combed
and braided her nervous dreams.

She will rock her mirror in a cradle,
never understood his heavy touch.

On this terrace anointed with dew
it was he who strained under insomnia,

the metal moon transfixing his mind.
Then he heard silence approaching as an army

down the taut roads. An emptiness blunts
the sheen and sharpness of things.

This furniture, that bridge, the whole valley
look slightly absurd, askew,

and about to melt. His devotion out east
will be forgotten.
                         Somewhere in the blue

distance a shepherd begins to sing.

TROY

When they tell you it's only a myth,
don't believe them.

When they say, oh yes, it does exist,
but as a relatively late settlement,
a vulgar Hellenistic town
shallowly buried in rough ground,
an unmade bed under a coverlet,
don't suppose it's all.

Schliemann came to this hill
in order to show that his boyhood
and Homeric Troy had both been real.

His proof of the child was identified
with knife-blades of silver, spear-tips of bronze
(their shafts had reverted to earth),
with soft gold calmly insisting
on feathery diadems like owls.

Ironically, the hoard was preheroic.

Missing Homer's tough city,
Schliemann found and founded his own.

Death, the tall duchess patiently waiting at Naples,
seemed trivial once he'd seen
that briskly successful businessman
becoming a mere negation, a husk,
concealing a robust boy.

Troy turned out to be many-layered,
a lavish birthday cake.
That level where Schliemann stood face to face
with himself at last had been burnt,
its rich crunchy texture containing

charcoal, blackened bricks, bones.
Each Troy is always liable to fall.

But don't suppose this is all.
You'll have to plunge deeper,
descend even steeper paths
past dark-blue strata, millennia,
and forget that sleekness of weapons,
those conveniences of wealth.

You'll want to plummet gently
but unerringly like amber in water
down to the first Troy, a slow
forgotten village where people
kept goats and gathered green walnuts
and nothing much ever happened,
get back to before the beginning, transcend
eras of flaming cities
or stupid adulthood.

POMPEII

There was something sham about it all.
Wood claimed to be marble. Crusted with cockle-shells
and blue glass, a cosy niche
only looked like a cave for nymphs. The orgies
rose unmessy, their S&M games
chic and slickly shocking to shopkeepers.

This culture is a massive example of kitsch.
Fourth-rate artists burst forth to imitate
pinnacled masters, their motifs and style.
Pigeons posed squeaky-clean,
apples lay docile. Afternoons were smothered
under store-bought sex and cheaply perfumed

oil. A boy scribbled on a wall:
"Here I've fucked many girls."
The despair, though, had a genuine slant
acknowledged too late to be helpful.
Moving like lava across their lawns,
history to the defeated says nothing at all.

CAESAR

I'm turning into pure movement and will,
a centrifugal urge, dreams of expansion.

I'm an arrow or spear, almost one-dimensional,
a keel splitting blue metal.

Years were silted up with delays,
bills chilled by the Senate.

Now I'm baring the blades of rivers: watch me.

But the space behind me fills
with women, a honey-blond warm wind
so strong I could lean back on it and rest.

I've whittled myself down to a few skills.

I'm also a Bronze Age king, garlanded
and robed, soberly, solemnly
fused with some brilliant Goddess, performing

tough tasks for his people until
he'll be killed in Her honour some spring.

Steel is tempered in cold water.

And I slope into sleep, a spilling over
down the hidden side of a hill.

With stars like perspiration on its forehead
my night-self waits, opening, then still,

ready to receive messages
from the dead or absent: masks
gazing stubbornly from a hazy sill.

Darkness defines my labours.
While I execute them the sun sings, shrill,
in a sky turquoise as Egyptian faience.

Boyhood fires of brass at night
steeply block-letter the stale news
that Troy has fallen. It always will.

My spirit is tempering this cold weather.

JULIUS CAESAR SPEAKS OF RIVERS

rivers are there to be crossed
                             don't care
about their linear tendency
                             ignore it

don't kill to get across, rather dedicate
live horses, mares with wild manes,
wide open white eyes
to the river god
                             let them loose
on demoralized marshland
                             let them shed
hard amber tears against your death

construct ingenious bridges
from whatever is the case
                             to its negation
let them span and soar above the bared
steel of water, wood
hammering hooves, yourself in scarlet
approaching that bank as if it were a woman
(pontifex maximus, greatest of bridge-makers)

and then pull the huge structure down

don't sail along a straight or meandering course
to the symbolic delta, wetland
with sweet and salt embracing, self-effacing,
and never trace a river to its source

don't foolishly follow borders
                             defy them

VI

STONE FIND

Concaved in stone,
this glossy flattened tassel
of silk isn't a sea-shell
or even a fossil.

It merely marks the place
where a mussel once nestled
under weaving Jurassic waters

long before long-haired girls
came along, longing for sea-food
and paleolithic true love.

This shard of shale
as a pillow preserves its indentation:
the Idea of *scallop,* no name
but a stylized Form.

THE PETRIFACTION

On my thirty-ninth birthday
I bought myself an amber bracelet
In the shop there is a stump
of petrified wood
It is forty million years old
It is pale as this paper,
looks brittle as a gingerbread
But with one finger-tip
I touched that block of stone
and felt it solid
Time itself, I thought, had coagulated
The pretty dappled rustling leaves
I found myself unable to imagine
Feeling very young,
I paid and left with my parcel

I dreamed that Nerissa,
my kitten aged four months,
was sitting on top of the stump
She is black like this print
There was a look of surprise
on her tiny teddy-bear face
It was the night after
my thirty-ninth birthday

VESTIGES

The crucial events of my life
will never be listed in the *Who's Who.*
They took place during your absences
or while you for a moment looked away.
They couldn't have been predicted or observed
or measured. Their moves were haphazard,
all interpretations remain my own.

Only some vestiges are possible to see
delicately trailed by invisible electrons
across this unpromising bubble-chamber.

TERRACOTTA

I'd like to construct a monument, round
and lasting as a terracotta pot.
Halfway between flesh and bread,

this *terre cuite*, baked earth,
glows red like humans under different skins.
For millennia our familiar, turned

on lathes or kneaded, such supple soil,
it emerged firmly from kilns
and filled with makers' breath.

Can't burn, won't rot,
squeaky-clean dirt around nails,
choir of inspired clay.

When vases made up their faces, jugs
put on weight, becoming cats.
Other skulls would prove

they could hold anything: food
or faeces, water or oil,
at last the puzzling ashes.
                                        Posed

as apples resembling breasts
resembling loaves, it never forgot
rainworms and that nervous system of roots,

pink brickdust when the sun goes down.

A MESOPOTAMIAN GLASS JAR

(C.I,500 B.C.)

Frail as peace of mind,
dark-brown like grief,
it outlasted Carthage
and Corinth, may outwit
    Mexico City.

Glass not blown but dipped,
a much older method,
soars raised now, a fist.
Fragments of the frieze run
    like a scar, convex.

The jar wasn't made to guard
rosed oil or balm:
this braid of swan-backed, slow
curls means *water* simply,
    absolute goodness.

THE GLASS APPLE

In dreams of apples
you plucked this object,
a moulded glass globe

which tempts with no September
scent, won't grow spotty,
shrivel or ferment.

Appledom essence,
it rests calmly,
massed on a shelf.

Possibly your breakfast
in that Other Orchard,
such green coolness claims

the name not of Knowledge
but a basic structure
grasped once and for all.

Hefty enough to kill with
and more of an apple
than those you simply eat,

it glows with perfection,
owes nothing to blossom
or any drastic Fall.

THE SNOW SCULPTURE

All day the children have been making ogres
and lanterns of sticky snow.
Candles are prettily lit at dusk.

Now, not to be outdone,
the fathers come. They build
a gigantic woman. She is kneeling,
naked, her hair hiding
both heels. Her breasts are melons
of edible wax. Snow crowns her.

One single flame is thickening
between her thighs, another
in her tiara of cream.

                    Come look at this fusion
of flimsy matter and robust form,
fire and frozen water,
urges of sex and mind.

A CRUCIAL EXPERIMENT

At that moment a wild hypothesis
was tested and found tenable:
light-rays from a distant star
would defect, get visibly deflected
near some huge gravitational centre
such as our sun.

There was no need for the concept of *force*.

Despite light's habit
of sticking to straight lines
the stellar beams were easily caught
in their weird act of bending,
a total solar eclipse
conceding the point debated.

Soon the experiment was rated a success.

Yes: I remember the years
when my own light was wrenched
off its true course
by your massive heaviness.

VII

MIGRATING HOOPERS

Their necks are a forest of trumpets.
These tough, unpretty birds
will rest an hour on the pond.

Dredging the recent past,
not even their silhouettes recall
reptile ancestors. The meeting

looks martial. Fanfares acknowledge
a triumph in progress, how all
have pressed on according to plan.

Or ballerinas wading in rubber boots
refuse to linger, won't languish,
melt in anguish among tulle,

then becoming ice-floes on a lake
unlocked, so palely blue
you'd think it white. Icebergs

are burning in the sky: a scent
of water penetrates your spirit.
And then the hoopers rise,

wish-bone formation aiming north.

SONG FOR A DEAD SEA-GULL

This is a rough linen death,
in winter fixed, by summer undecided.
The bale of dry decay was left untended
weathering severe seasons.

This death was left feathered
but deftly tacked to soil
with sixty green stitches
preempting burial.

Compose a song left unended.
The carcass is worn as cloth.
Rains have cut out at last
this patch of turf to float on the canal.

One canvas wing unfolding and the wind
improbably set sail.
This is a death uncaught and undefined,
a life left open-ended.

MAGPIES IN MIDWINTER

Silently like feathered fruit
they dapple a solstice garden.
No laughter breaks the spell

of concerns. When the sun drops
from its branch they consider deaths,
territorial rights, youngsters

to match, newcomers hatched,
thriving or snatched by gangsters.
Appling bared trees

these dapper birds plan to thatch
or mend homes, applying
the tenderness of curved lines.

Christmas glass balls flash
heavily, white and green-tinged
black. But horse-chestnuts bear buds

humans don't notice.
Duly the magpies perform.
They think winter is an egg.

SNAKES

two baby boas in a perspex box
trace graceful arabesques on sand
hang lank as wool or wet spaghetti
fron a dead desert branch
burnished into pewter

among their cacti, pebbles and rocks
both need that body heat, blood beat
they can't themselves produce

I think: "these are the healing holy serpents
wound around Hermes' wand"

they work from ten to six
decorating a shop-window
attracting customers:
in the background some young women will try on
second-hand skirts of pastel tulle
sequined and flounced

snakes: longing to be near
somebody calm and warm

these gentle, easy-going creatures
that eat their live mice twice a week
lap milk from a chipped saucer

one at a time the boas take
their daily bath
in a bone-yellow bowl of water,
submerge coil upon coil
till they lie tidily curled up
like the spring of a mechanical watch

its eyes contracted into glittering slits,
only the head pokes up, a periscope:

77

prettily, placidly the jaws become a yawn

an image of pure hedonism

snakes: patterned with *petit point*
the colours of basalt and tin
snakes: collapsed in a love-heap,
trickling as treacle over stone
or elegantly draped in drooping loops

and dreaming like myself of human skin

*Note. Unlike Asclepius, Hermes is not a god of
healing, but it is he who carries the caduceus, or
wand with two serpents. Asclepius' rod has only one
as a rule. I believe, however, that these were
originally identical, and that Asclepius inherited
his from Hermes.*

VIII

GOODBYE TO THE BERLIN WALL

unlike China's Great Wall
stitched along six united kingdoms
and unlike Hadrian's Wall
a selvage of empire
it offered no protection

ours is an age when old walls
crumble, tumble down
ours is an age of transcendence

I was born into a post-war world
of walls, fences, thresholds, barbed wire,
maps lined and scarred like faces

of abstract concepts too rigidly defined
differences falsely presented as opposites
fanatically excluding each other

an Iron Curtain fell brutally
like the knife-blade of a guillotine
or long like a shadow at sunset
or drastically
like darkness in the tropics

as a child I saw a literal iron curtain
how it slowly, creakingly descended, then rose,
a precaution against fire
ladybird-red tulips and pea-green grass
were painted on the dull metal surface
as a concession to prettiness

I believed that the other Iron Curtain
looked just the same
but there was a lovelier one, the mint-green
Bamboo Curtain, semi-transparent
and patterned with undulating shadows,

branches and snakes,
perhaps also a Silk Curtain, softly rustling,
with a row of slippered feet
comically showing beneath

and I remembered a horrifying story
about an iron curtain that dropped on an actor:
both split and had to be replaced

Europe had been cut in two like Snow-White's apple,
one half was red, the other almost beige
"you take that part, I keep this"
whispered the wicked witch

but now we have reached
an age of transgression

and the apple was wax or wood, too round,
too glossy to be true,
an object discovered, covered with dust,
in some stage properties room;
an object forgotten, then found,
a collector's item today

close to the Wall
there was a mulberry tree whose berries
fell and left menstrual stains
there was also a powder-blue moon:
it sank, leaving nothing behind
there were two desperate lovers
kissing through a chink

ours is an age when traditional boundaries
are criticized, questioned

so why are we still interested in division,
distinctions, differences,
still high on Plato's metaphysics

and Aristotle's logic

all this splitting of skulls
all this polarization of concepts

this is me, that is you,
this is mine, that is yours

Eliot's curtain of falling blood

but individual bricks from the Berlin Wall
are now preserved like bars of gold;
its lumps of grey gritty concrete
are set in silver and sold
expensively as jewellery

the Wild West concept of *frontier*
is beautiful because fluid, liquid
and denoting something equally fluid, liquid,
a never-fixed boundary
an ever-receding horizon

yes: we visited this Wall once
the way one visits a tomb
but I was dressed in white,
and small rowans, dry moss, blades of grass
grew between the bricks:
what we saw had already become
an ancient monument
two border guards in a tall tower waved
and we waved back;
it was my birthday:
in West Berlin we had cream cake
plenty of cake and plenty of cream
like a naïve dream about the opulent West

too much dwelling on differences
"disturbs the unity of the mind"

asserted Virginia Woolf

old borderlines slashed the world and left
long marks in grass

luminously blue at nightfall
and near the Wall there were crosses,
tiny, pathetic, like those planted
on graves of pets

a curtain of falling tears

this absurd Wall has at long last
accomplished its historic mission
(don't ask me what it was),
risen and made its exit

ours is an age of passage,
the crossing of rivers, blurring of borders

don't tell me this, I know:
East Europeans won't only accept
our democracy
but also our hamburger stands and soap operas
and discover the degrees of our freedom,
how much it costs,
and that one's greed always exceeds one's grasp

do you think Romania's sheep will turn white?
their dark fleeces aren't natural but due to pollution

a curtain of falling soot

now that the Wall is gone,
the Curtain up
don't let's go on pigeon-holing each other:
it isn't just wrong, it's tedious,
this frantic looking for what's unfamiliar

this mania for marking boundaries
the lovers are finally free to embrace,
to go wherever they like
they're not ridiculous, not even histrionic
but simply themselves:
believe me, they will survive

                                    1990

THE GULF WAR 1991 AS TV ENTERTAINMENT

How eerily beautiful it looks, this war,
outlined against coral-pale sunsets and dawns.

How lovely the very names employed:
"Jerusalem" is gold and silver, an alloy,

"Baghdad" a topaz cut into a dome.
Desert Storm offers a suitable trope,

a Mirage soars incarnate in metal and glass.
Tomcats and Wild Weasels dart off really fast.

When the sun drops sharply, a copper coin,
I'm tuned in to that muffled monotonous noise

of older conflicts among the same rocks
where creeds like borders converge and cross.

Spirits of air ascend, then descend,
their brief embraces blazing white and red.

Huge chrysanthemums of precious stones
emerge out of darkness just when they explode.

I remember that my body is a satin tent
hurriedly raised for a few hours' rest.

This mercury has plunged abruptly like the sun.
Night is a purple rectangle tinged with mud.

Next morning a dying cormorant, sleeked
by an oil slick, will quietly contradict the dream.